# HURRICANES

## EARTH'S MIGHTIEST STORMS

# HURRICANES

## EARTH'S MIGHTIEST STORMS

### by Patricia Lauber

SCHOLASTIC INC.
New York  Toronto  London  Auckland  Sydney

The maps and diagrams were created by Gary Tong, using airbrush, watercolor, and color pencil. Photo research by Donna Frankland and Zoe Moffitt. Design by Sylvia Frezzolini Severance.

ISBN 0-590-47407-3

Copyright © 1996 by Patricia Lauber. All rights reserved. Published by Scholastic Inc. SCHOLASTIC and associated logos are trademarks and/or registered trademarks of Scholastic Inc.

20 19 18 17 16 15 14                            2/0
Printed in the U.S.A.                           08

*Galveston, Texas, was built on a low-lying island between Galveston Bay and the Gulf of Mexico. On the morning of September 8, 1900, it was a bustling port city of 40,000 people. By midnight, winds and waves of a gigantic hurricane had pounded half the city into rubble and killed 6,000 people in the worst storm disaster of U.S. history.*

# CONTENTS

*Before the days of satellites, ships at sea often provided the first news of great storms with gale winds and gigantic waves.*

# A Monster Storm

The storm was born sometime in late summer of 1938, somewhere in tropical waters of the North Atlantic Ocean. No one saw it. No one tracked it. At that time weather satellites did not exist, and no ship happened near the young storm. Unseen and unknown, it began a long journey.

Winds nudged and shoved the storm westward across the Atlantic. As it traveled, the storm fed on warm, moist air. It grew into a huge mass of dark clouds. Within the clouds, lightning crackled, thunder crashed, and strong winds howled. Sheets of rain fell. Still unseen, the powerful storm was whirling toward North America. By the time it drew near, it was a full-fledged hurricane, carrying winds of at least 75 miles an hour.

First word of the storm came by radio on September 16, after a Brazilian freighter met hurricane winds and heavy seas northeast of Puerto Rico. Reports from other ships followed.

At the United States Weather Bureau in Jacksonville, Florida, weather scientists began fitting reports together. They soon learned that a monster hurricane was bearing down on Florida. Unless it changed course, it would strike near Miami on the evening of Tuesday, September 20. They issued an urgent hurricane warning.

In and around Miami, people boarded up windows, doubled mooring lines on their boats, and laid in supplies of food, water, batteries, and candles. They knew how to get ready. The past ten years had brought them 11 hurricanes and ten storms of near-hurricane strength.

But the hurricane did not strike. By Monday night, it had turned north. Everyone relaxed.

The storm seemed to be following a path taken by many other hurricanes. It would move north toward Cape Hatteras, North Carolina, then turn east, dying out over cool water. The national weather map for Wednesday, September 21, did not even show a hurricane, just a storm moving out to sea. Yet the truth was that no one really knew where the hurricane was or what it was doing.

No one knew that the hurricane was still headed north, that it had not turned out to sea.

No one knew that the hurricane had picked up speed. It was no longer traveling at 20 miles an hour. It was roaring along at 60 or 70, as fast as a tornado.

No one knew that the whirling winds within the storm were gusting to 200 miles an hour.

No one knew that the hurricane was barreling toward the Northeast coast. Even as the edge of the storm was tearing up boardwalks and piers along the New Jersey shore, no warnings were sent ahead.

The people of Long Island and New England had no reason to expect anything worse than some stormy weather. No giant hurricane had struck the region in 123 years, since September 23, 1815.

The south shore of Long Island faces the Atlantic. It is sheltered only by islands of sand called barrier beaches. Along these beaches, people had built everything from summer cottages to large houses. Westhampton Beach, for instance, had 179 houses on a strip of sand that was ten miles long and a quarter of a mile wide. This barrier beach stood squarely in the path of the storm that no one was expecting.

Because it was early fall, most of the summer people had gone home. Those still at the beach were awed by the size of the ocean waves on the morning of Wednesday, September 21. A few even called friends and invited them to drive out over the bridge and see the waves.

In early afternoon, winds struck. Deck chairs and shutters swooped through the air like leaves. Roof shingles rippled and tore loose. Windows blew in, doors blew open. The sky turned black. Telephone poles snapped. Rain fell in sheets, sweeping through broken windows and open doors. Water crept up around houses. Then the sea struck.

*The town of Westhampton was littered with wreckage of its own and from Westhampton Beach. The big house at right rode out the storm. The one at left was torn from its foundation.*

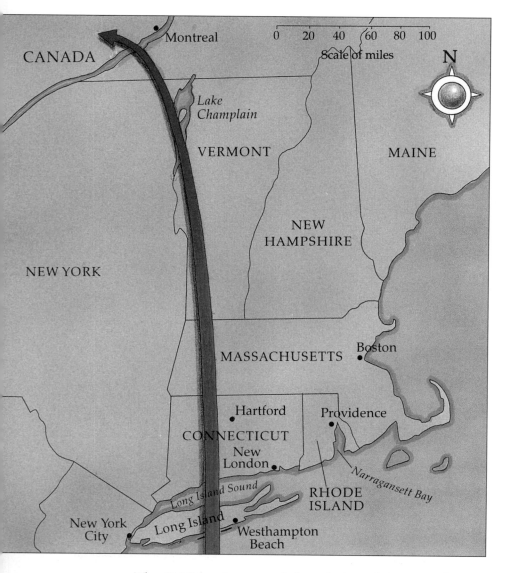

*The 1938 hurricane traveled north through New England into Canada.*

Three hours before high tide, water reached the high-tide mark. Then came a wall of water that appeared to be 40 feet high — a storm surge. People who saw the storm surge thought it was a thick bank of fog rolling in, but it wasn't fog. It was water, water that crushed and swept away everything in its path. Cottages crumbled. Whole houses were lifted off their foundations and smashed to pieces.

Terrified by the wind and rain that came before the surge, some people had fled across the bridge. Many were too late. Caught up by the storm surge, they swam for their lives. The lucky ones scrambled onto floating roofs or doors that served as rafts. Hours later they washed ashore.

Meanwhile, the hurricane was charging across Long Island. The people in its path felt trapped in a nightmare from which they could not wake. The world had become unreal. Water swallowed houses. Roofs blew off. Pianos flew through the air. Birds, racing to escape, appeared to be flying backward.

Rising water drove people from the first floor of their houses to the second to the attic. Then houses collapsed. Boats tore loose and crashed into other boats and bridges. Trees fell. Church steeples toppled. And through it all, the only sound that could be heard was the howl of the wind: sometimes a scream, sometimes a deep bass, but mostly a pulsing groan.

The hurricane rushed on across Long Island Sound to Connecticut. The city of New London lay in its path. Wind and waves smashed the waterfront with its boats, docks, buildings. Then somehow fire broke out. Winds whipped the fire until the whole waterfront was ablaze. With telephone lines down, messengers struggled on

*Wrecked boats and wharves lined the waterfront of New London.*

*Swept ashore, the lighthouse tender* Tulip *lies across the railroad tracks in New London.*

foot to the fire department. Firemen were slow to respond because streets were blocked by fallen trees and telephone poles. When they finally turned their hoses on the fires, wind blew the water back at them. At one time it seemed the whole city would burn. Then the wind shifted. Fires were blown back at areas that had already burned. With no fresh fuel, they died out.

Much of the Connecticut shore was spared a storm surge because Long Island acted as a breakwater, where the surge spent itself. Rhode Island had no breakwater.

Rhode Islanders did have a warning of hurricane winds and heavy rain. But with telephone lines down all over Long Island, no word of the storm surge had spread.

At one moment, people at Misquamicut were joking and putting up storm shutters. The next moment, their houses were under 30 feet of water. Forty-one people picnicking on the beach

*Wind and water stalled this Boston-bound train near Stonington, Connecticut. Most passengers escaped when the train crew herded them into the first car and the engine. The crew uncoupled the rest of the train and edged forward to safety.*

were swept away. After the storm, Misquamicut looked as if no one had ever set foot there.

At Napatree Point, in Watch Hill, every house washed away. Survivors rode the wreckage to shore hours later.

Providence, capital of Rhode Island, stands at the head of Narragansett Bay, 30 miles from the Atlantic. The storm surge raged up the bay, snatched the lighthouse from Whale Rock, hurled 20-ton boulders in the air, and, as the bay narrowed, rose higher and higher. By the time it reached the head of the bay, the storm surge was a mountain of water carrying boats and houses that became battering rams.

Rushing water crushed the docks at the head of the bay. Hundreds of boats were torn from their moorings, slammed against one another, and turned into splinters.

In downtown Providence, office workers were getting ready to go home when they looked out their windows and saw that the city was full of water. It rose to the height of first-floor ceilings, trapping people in shops and restaurants. The sea took on an eerie glow as it swallowed automobiles with their headlights on.

*The storm surge swamped downtown Providence in eight to ten feet of water. Note people clustered on steps of the city hall, escaping from the flooded streets.*

Windows burst, and broken glass was driven through the air. Chimneys crumbled in showers of bricks around people clinging to cars, lampposts, and trees.

The hurricane sped up the Connecticut River valley, tearing off roofs, shattering shop windows, felling trees, flattening crops. With rain falling in torrents, streams swelled and burst over their banks, flooding towns. Along the Connecticut River, volunteers labored in the wind and rain to

*Along the hurricane's path, streams and rivers swelled to overflowing. In Rockville, Connecticut, as elsewhere, volunteers stacked sandbags to prevent flooding. Note that the water has risen higher than the land.*

*A church steeple, 165 feet high, toppled in Danielson, Connecticut. The wind was blowing so hard that two men had to hold up the photographer.*

stack sandbags, hoping to keep the river within its banks. At Hartford, capital of Connecticut, the river rose 33 feet above normal.

There were places where the river was held back. In other places it jumped its banks and spread over fields and lawns into houses. Though the hurricane had rushed on north, the flooding went on for two days, as water drained into the river and rushed downstream.

The city of Boston was on the fringe of the storm, but it was shaken by winds of more than 100 miles an hour. At the airport, winds knocked down the radio tower and tossed an eight-ton airplane into a salt marsh half a mile away.

Mount Washington, the highest point in New England, registered winds of 190 miles an hour. Lesser winds toppled whole forests in the mountains of Vermont and New Hampshire.

Turning slightly west, the hurricane howled over Lake Champlain, crumpling cottages and hurling boats ashore. So much rain fell that the whole lake rose two feet.

By 11:00 P.M. the storm had crossed into Canada and was hammering Montreal. Its winds dropped, but they still did widespread damage.

*In Stonington, Connecticut, the storm tore boats from their moorings and parked them on the shore.*

A little more than eight hours after its first landfall on the barrier beaches of Long Island, the hurricane finally died out over Canada.

In those few hours, more than 600 people died. Another 63,000 lost their homes. Countless automobiles and boats were destroyed. All along the storm's path, crops and livestock were wiped out, as were forests. Some 20,000 miles of telephone and electric wires were down. Rail service between New York and Boston halted until crews could rebuild bridges and remove hundreds of trees and telephone poles from the tracks — as well as houses, yachts, and a 300-foot-long steamboat. The U.S. Post Office borrowed a battleship from the Navy to haul mail between the two cities.

With the passing of the storm, weather scientists began trying to understand what had happened. How and why had this monster of a storm reached Long Island and New England?

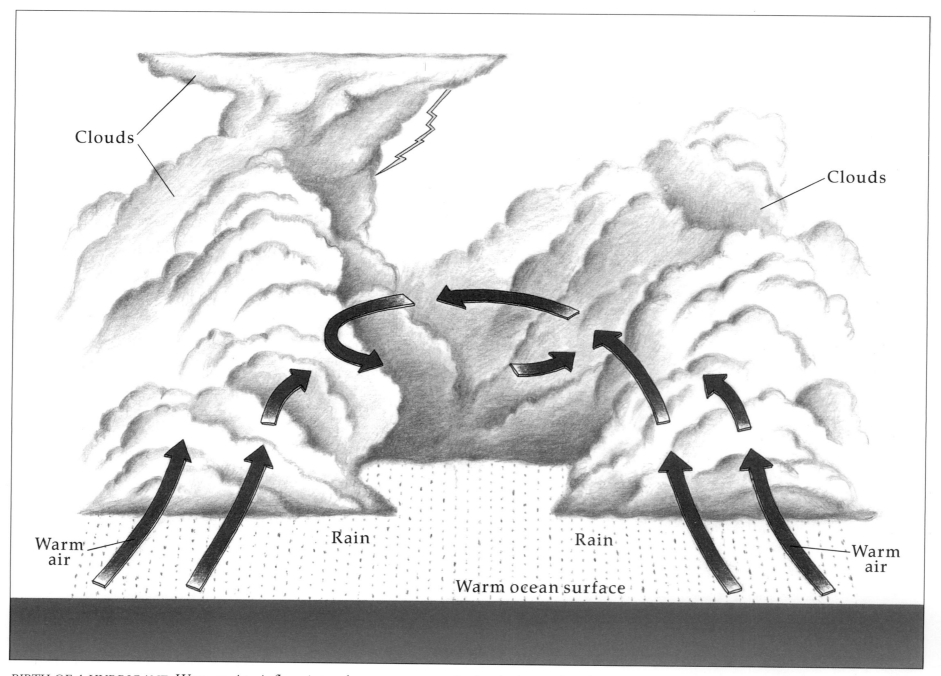

*BIRTH OF A HURRICANE: Warm, moist air flows into a low-pressure area. As the air rises and condenses into clouds, more warm air is drawn in over the surface of the ocean. It spirals upwards, traveling counterclockwise. Clusters of thunderstorms form.*

# THE MAKING OF A HURRICANE

Great whirling storms roar out of the oceans in many parts of the world. They are called by several names — hurricane, typhoon, and cyclone are the three most familiar ones. But no matter what they are called, they are all the same sort of storm. They are born the same way, in tropical waters. They develop the same way, feeding on warm, moist air. And they do the same kind of damage, both ashore and at sea. Other storms may cover a bigger area or have higher winds, but none can match both the size and the fury of hurricanes. They are earth's mightiest storms.

Like all storms, they take place in the atmosphere, the envelope of air that surrounds the earth and presses on its surface. The pressure at any one place is always changing. There are days when air is sinking and the atmosphere presses harder on the surface. These are times of high pressure.

There are days when a lot of air is rising and the atmosphere does not press down as hard. These are times of low pressure. Low-pressure areas over warm oceans give birth to hurricanes.

No one knows exactly what happens to start these storms. But when conditions are right, warm, moist air is set in motion. It begins to rise rapidly from the surface of the ocean in a low-pressure area.

Like water in a hose, air flows from where there is more pressure to where there is less pressure. And so air over the surface of the ocean flows into the low-pressure area, picking up moisture as it travels. This warm, moist air soars upward.

As the air rises above the earth, it cools. The cooling causes moisture to condense into tiny droplets of water that form clouds. As the moisture condenses, it gives off heat. Heat is one kind of energy. It is the energy that powers the storm. The clouds are the source of the storm's rain.

The low-pressure area acts like a chimney — warm air is drawn in at the bottom, rises in a column, cools, and spreads out. As the air inside rises and more air is drawn in, the storm grows.

The air being drawn in, however, does not travel in a straight line. The earth's surface is rotating, and the rotation causes the path to curve. The air travels in a spiral within the storm. In the Northern Hemisphere, the spiraling winds travel counterclockwise — the opposite of the way the hands of a clock move. In the Southern Hemisphere, they travel clockwise.

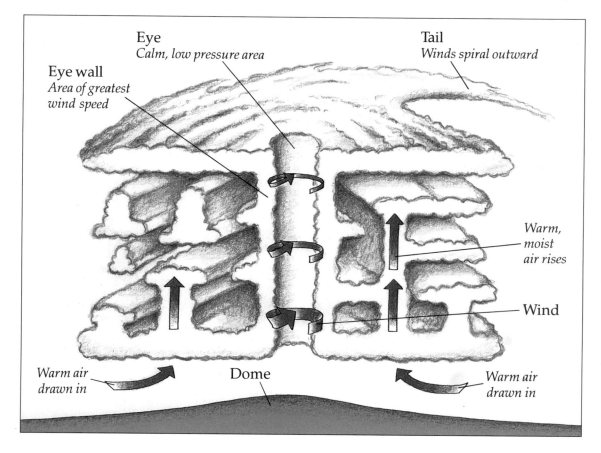

Eye
*Calm, low pressure area*

Tail
*Winds spiral outward*

Eye wall
*Area of greatest wind speed*

Warm, moist air rises

Wind

Warm air drawn in

Dome

Warm air drawn in

*INSIDE A HURRICANE: High winds spiral around the eye, but within the eye all is calm. Air pressure within the eye is extremely low. Because there is less pressure on it than on surrounding areas, the sea under the hurricane rises in a bulge, or dome.*

20

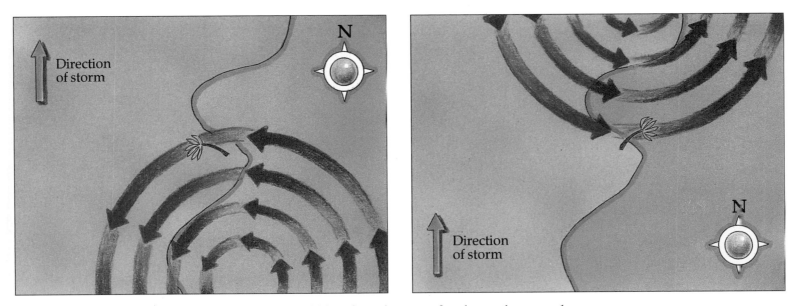

*If hurricane winds first blow from the east, they will blow from the west after the eye has passed.*

Most of these storms die out within hours or days of their birth. Only about one out of ten grows into a hurricane.

As high winds develop, air pressure falls rapidly at the center of the storm. This low-pressure area is called the eye, and it may be ten to 20 miles across. The eye is a hole that reaches from bottom to top of the storm. Winds rage around the hole, but within it all is calm. Winds are light. The air is clear, with blue sky or scattered clouds and sunshine above. People caught in a hurricane may suddenly experience calm air and dry skies. Sometimes they make the mistake of thinking the storm has ended, but it hasn't. The eye moves on and the second half of the storm arrives, with winds blowing from the opposite direction.

The storm of 1938 began as a low-pressure area, probably in a region where hurricanes are often born — somewhere off the west coast of Africa. Here ocean waters are 80 degrees Fahrenheit or warmer.

Winds carried the growing storm westward. The winds were produced by a huge high-pressure area called the Bermuda High, which blankets part of the North Atlantic. These winds travel in a clockwise direction and they usually steer an Atlantic hurricane.

Most often the winds wheel a storm north as it approaches North America. By the time it reaches Cape Hatteras, the winds are wheeling it east, away from land. But this does not always happen. A storm may tear up islands in the Caribbean or come ashore in Florida. It may swing into the Gulf of Mexico and make its landing as far west as Texas or Mexico. Or it may move north to Georgia and the Carolinas.

The 1938 hurricane did none of these things. One reason was that the Bermuda High was not where it was supposed to be. Normally it is centered over the North Atlantic in September. In 1938 it had drifted nearly 1,000 miles and was centered off Newfoundland.

*In September the Bermuda High is normally centered over the North Atlantic. Its winds carry hurricanes westward across the ocean and may also steer them away from land. In 1938 that did not happen.*

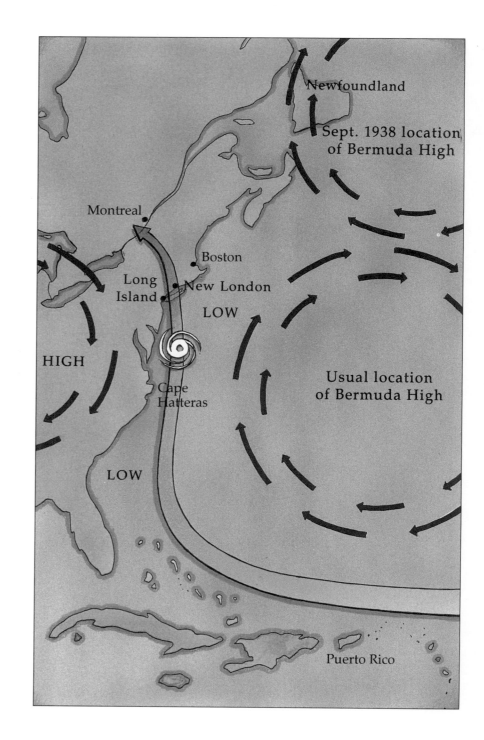

A second reason was that a band of low pressure stretched from Cape Hatteras through New England. The band was trapped between two high-pressure areas, one to the east and one to the west. New England had had four days of warm, wet weather. More was forecast for September 21.

The band of low pressure formed a natural path for the hurricane to take. The hurricane took it. Barreling along like an express train, it bore down on Long Island and the barrier beaches.

Tides would have been high anyway, because this was a time when the sun and moon were lined up with the earth. Their combined pull causes very high tides. The incoming tide was two feet higher than normal, even without the storm. Now hurricane winds added to the tide by blowing masses of water against the shore and holding them there.

But the storm surge was far worse than the flooding caused by winds and tide. A surge is a bulge in the ocean under a hurricane. Where air pressure is very low, the ocean rises, forming a bulge or dome. When the surge reaches shallow water near shore, it is slowed. It may then rise

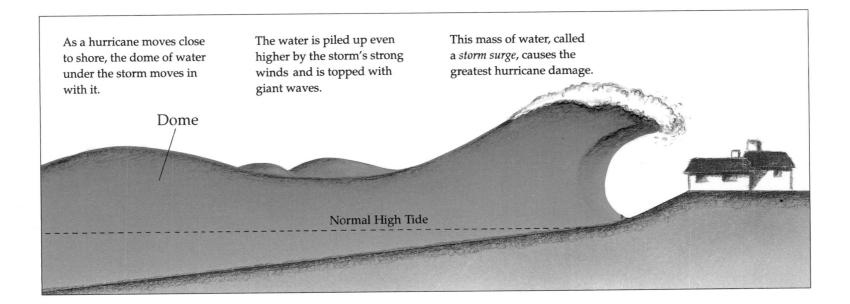

As a hurricane moves close to shore, the dome of water under the storm moves in with it.

The water is piled up even higher by the storm's strong winds and is topped with giant waves.

This mass of water, called a *storm surge*, causes the greatest hurricane damage.

Dome

Normal High Tide

*As the 1938 storm traveled north, swollen rivers tore out bridges in towns like Waterville, Massachusetts.*

even higher, as it did in 1938, because the water piles up. A storm surge can do more damage than any other part of a hurricane.

An extra-high tide and a storm surge topped by wind-driven waves — when all this water broke over land, it crushed the houses of Westhampton Beach, swept clean the beaches of Rhode Island, and flooded Providence.

The winds in the first part of the hurricane were blowing from the southeast. Once the eye had passed, they blew from the northwest. This was the change in wind direction that put out the fires in New London, blowing the flames back toward areas that had already burned.

In most hurricanes, water does the greatest damage, but not all that water comes from the ocean. The 1938 storm arrived after four days of rain in New England. Now more rain fell in torrents. In the Connecticut River valley the ground was already wet. It could not absorb more rain. Water rushed down hills, and low-lying areas became lakes. Water rushed into streams and rivers, which swelled and overflowed their banks. City storm drains filled and streets flooded.

The same four days of rain helped the storm travel as far as Montreal. Along the hurricane's path there was plenty of warm, moist air to feed on. Only when it reached cool land north of Montreal did the storm come to an end.

Weather scientists learned a lot as they worked out what had happened on September 21, 1938. They also set a goal: to make sure that no big storm would ever again come as a terrifying surprise. In time, they would succeed. But first they needed a better understanding of hurricanes and better tools for studying the storms. In 1938 their tools were ones that forecasters had been using for several hundred years.

# Some Weather Instruments

Ancient peoples lived through great storms. They looked for signs that would help them predict the weather. They tried to explain the weather they experienced. But no one can really study weather without measuring what is happening. The instruments to make such measurements were invented three to four hundred years ago. Modern versions of them are still used today.

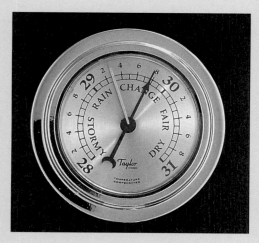

### BAROMETER
*A barometer measures air pressure. Rising air pressure tells of fair weather, while falling pressure tells of stormy weather. This kind of barometer is often seen in homes and schools.*

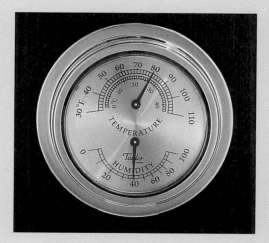

### HYGROMETER
*A hygrometer measures the amount of moisture in the air: the humidity. Warm air can hold more moisture, or water vapor, than cool or cold air. When warm, moist air is cooled, water vapor condenses, changing from a gas to a liquid. That is why a glass of ice-cold soda seems to sweat in summer — warm air around the glass is chilled and water vapor condenses out of it onto the glass.*

### ANEMOMETER
*An anemometer measures wind speed. The rate at which its blades spin outdoors is registered on a dial indoors. In the 1938 hurricane and other violent storms, anemometers have blown away, making it hard to tell what the highest wind speeds were.*

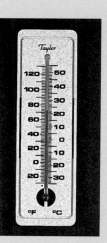

### THERMOMETER
*A thermometer measures temperature.*

# World Names

In the Caribbean Sea and North Atlantic, earth's mightiest storms are called *hurricanes*, after a Carib Indian word for "big wind." In the Pacific they are also called hurricanes if they occur east of the international dateline. West of the dateline they are called *typhoons*, from Chinese words for "great wind." In the Indian Ocean they are called *cyclones*, an English name based on a Greek word meaning "coil," as in "coil of a snake," because of the winds that spiral within them. The storms also have a number of local names. Many Australians, for example, call them *willy-willies*. The name probably began as "whirlwind," which became "whirly-whirly," which became "willy-willy."

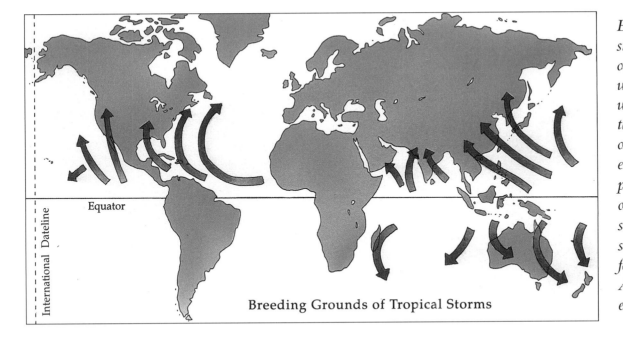

Equator

International Dateline

**Breeding Grounds of Tropical Storms**

*Earth's mightiest storms take shape over tropical waters. All move westward at first, then either die out over land or turn eastward, losing power over cooler ocean waters. For some reason, these storms do not form in the South Atlantic or south-east Pacific oceans.*

*As time passed, hurricane-hunting planes became flying laboratories, capable of recording many kinds of information. This U.S. Air Force plane was at work during the hurricane season of 1963.*

# INTO THE EYE OF THE STORM

Toward the end of World War II, a United States fleet was twice badly damaged by typhoons in the Pacific because of poor weather forecasts. One result was that Army and Navy planes were ordered to start tracking and studying hurricanes.

As it happened, some studies were already under way. A year earlier, an Army Air Force instructor had flown in and out of a hurricane. His flight opened up a new way to study the great storms.

The instructor believed that with proper training a pilot could fly in any kind of weather. In late July of 1943, he learned that a hurricane was nearing Galveston, Texas. With a navigator, he took off in a single-engine trainer and flew over the Gulf of Mexico into the storm.

At the edge of the storm, the small plane bucked in strong winds. Driving rain enveloped it. Dark clouds blotted out light. As the fliers pressed on, hurricane winds tossed the plane up and down and sideways in a roller-coaster ride. Suddenly the plane was surrounded by calm. They were in the eye of the storm. Above was blue sky. Below was the Texas landscape. Then the black clouds closed in and winds again seized the little plane as it chewed its way through the other side of the storm and out into clear weather.

By late 1945, Army and Navy planes had made hundreds of flights into the mightiest storms on earth. Weather scientists were learning what takes place inside a hurricane. With reports from hurricane-hunting planes, they could tell where an eye was and how fast it was moving.

Today rugged planes carry many instruments

into hurricanes as they near land. The instruments measure winds, temperatures, and humidity. They measure the water content of clouds. They photograph the inside of hurricanes. They record radar images of the storms.

In April 1960, the first weather satellite rocketed into orbit. Now scientists hoped to find and track tropical storms before they neared land. They were rewarded almost at once. A few days after its launching, the satellite discovered a typhoon in the South Pacific.

Satellite instruments do not see into the heart of a hurricane — that work is still done by planes. Satellites show the size of the storm and its growth. They show changes in the size of the eye: if the eye is growing bigger, the storm is weakening; if it is growing smaller, the storm is strengthening. Most important, satellites can pinpoint the location of a storm, record its speed, and track it closely.

Information from ground stations and ships,

*The United States is launching a new series of satellites that will help scientists track and predict the paths of storms.*

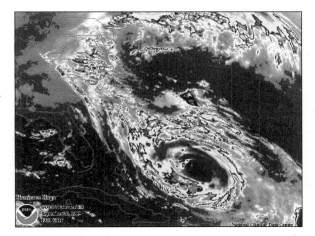

*September 20, 9:31 A.M.*

*September 20, 9:31 P.M.*

*September 21, 10:01 A.M.*

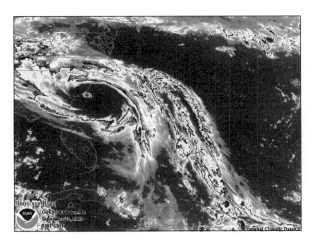

*September 21, 11:01 P.M.*

*September 22, 1:01 A.M.*

*September 22, 11:01 A.M.*

*Satellite images track Hurricane Hugo as it sweeps through the Caribbean to South Carolina in 1989.*

*Information about Hurricane Andrew flows into the National Hurricane Center in 1992.*

from hurricane-hunting planes and satellites — forecasters have more information than the human mind can grasp. But since the 1960s, they have been able to feed all this information into computers. Now they can create computer models of hurricanes. They can compare a hurricane with similar ones that occurred years earlier. Forecasting just one storm may involve several million bits of data and several billion mathemat-ical calculations. Huge computers do the work.

Today no one who reads a newspaper, listens to radio, or watches television can be taken by surprise when a hurricane strikes. Although forecasters cannot say exactly where a hurricane will come ashore, they do know which areas will feel the storm. They can warn people in its path, as they did with Andrew in the summer of 1992.

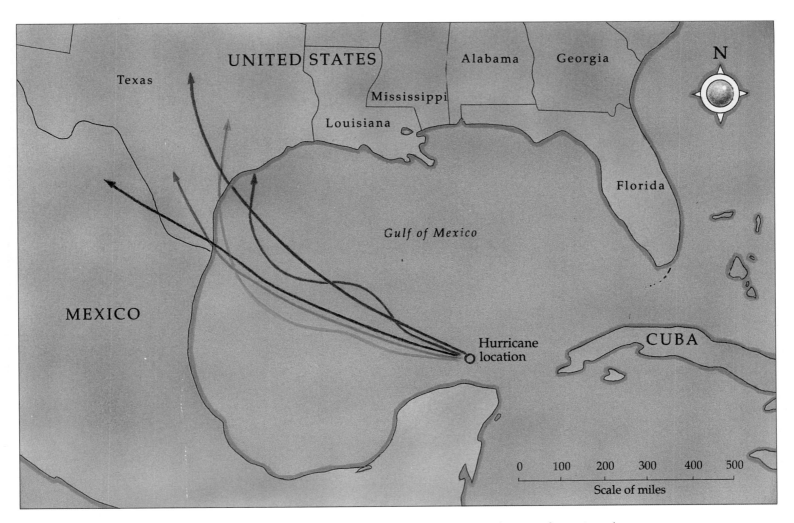

Computers work with millions of pieces of stored information about past storms and new information about an approaching storm. Each is programmed to compare and select facts and then predict what the hurricane will do and where it will make its landfall. But hurricanes are likely to behave in unexpected ways, and so far no one can say for sure exactly where a storm will come ashore. The colored lines on this map show how four computer programs predicted the path of one hurricane. The black line shows the storm's actual path.

*From high above the earth, shuttle astronauts looked down at Typhoon Pat and its clearly defined eye in the West Pacific Ocean.*

# Naming Hurricanes

In the 1800s only the most violent hurricanes were named, sometimes for a town or an island that was badly damaged. Most of these names were used only locally.

Once it became possible to track tropical storms and hurricanes, weather scientists needed a way to identify them. Starting in 1953, the first tropical storm of the season was given a woman's name starting with A, the second a woman's name starting with B, and so on through the alphabet. In 1979, men's names were added to the list of those used.

Names repeat every six years. But if a storm is particularly violent, its name may be taken off the list. Camille and Hugo, for example, are no longer used. Hurricane Camille means only the storm that swept the Mississippi Delta in 1969, and Hugo the storm that battered the Virgin Islands, Puerto Rico, and Charleston, South Carolina, in 1989.

Different sets of names are used for different parts of the world. Hurricanes that form within 1,000 miles of Hawaii, for example, are given Hawaiian names.

*Hurricane Andrew came ashore in South Florida during the early morning hours of August 24, 1992.*

# Big Winds and Big Damage

In mid-August of 1992, satellite pictures showed a low-pressure area of wind and rain moving west across the Atlantic. Though the storm did not seem to amount to much, the National Hurricane Center in Miami, Florida, tracked it carefully.

By August 20 the storm was about 400 miles east of Puerto Rico. Here it weakened so much that it almost disappeared. The lower part of the storm was moving northwest, but the upper part was being blown northeast by strong high-altitude winds. For a time, it seemed the storm might be torn apart. Instead, the high-altitude winds began to flow around the storm. It charged ahead, with all its parts moving in the same direction.

By then scientists at the Hurricane Center were working with computer models of storms. They were trying to predict the storm's behavior and decide whether people should be told to leave coastal areas. The scientists fed their computers all the data they had received from satellites, radar, and airplane flights into the storm.

By 4:00 A.M. of August 22, winds within the storm were blowing at more than 75 miles an hour. The storm had become a hurricane. First of the season, it was named Andrew.

As its winds swirled ever faster, Andrew churned across the Bahamas. It was a furious and compact storm, with an eye only eight miles wide and winds that reached out for 60 miles. It was heading for the east coast of Florida.

The computer models could not predict exactly where Andrew would come ashore. For

250 miles, from Fort Lauderdale to Key West, people were ordered to evacuate all low-lying areas along the coast.

Sunday, August 23, dawned clear and fair in south Florida. The sky was blue with fleecy clouds. Temperatures rose into the 90s. The air was damp and salty. Herons and frigate birds drifted over blue waters. It could have been any summer day, except that roads were jammed with cars as people fled inland and north.

By evening, wind and sea were rising. Shortly after midnight, in the early hours of August 24, Andrew came ashore south of Miami, with winds gusting to 195 miles an hour.

People woke in terror to dark houses, without electricity. The wind, sometimes shrieking, sometimes growling like a rushing freight train, snatched at shutters and shingles and pounded the sides of houses. Walls bulged in, then out. Howling winds toppled trees, ripped off roofs, blew in windows and doors, and knocked down houses. Where roofs or walls were gone, rain poured in. Inside their houses, people huddled together, held hands, and prayed.

The eye of the storm passed quickly through, bringing only minutes of calm and silence. Then the second half of the storm arrived, with winds howling from the opposite direction.

Moving west, Andrew cut a 25-mile-wide path through Everglades National Park, flattening trees, tearing out boardwalks, and leveling the visitors center.

The storm moved out over the Gulf of Mexico and made a second landfall, west of Baton Rouge, Louisiana, where it died out over the swamps and marshes.

The sun rose on a strange landscape. In Miami large boats, hurled ashore, now leaned against lampposts and lay across highways. Wind had stripped the signs off posts and the fronds off palm trees. Fallen trees, telephone poles, and cables blocked streets. Traffic lights had disappeared.

But Miami had been at the edge of the hurricane. The center of the storm had hit to the south, bulldozing the towns of Homestead and Florida City. Twenty miles inland, they had been

*The towns of Homestead and Florida City were crushed by Andrew's winds.*

People were stunned by the destruction, which cost them their homes and most of their possessions.

crushed not by the sea but by the wind. They looked as if they had been bombed, and 22 people had died.

The people in this area were not wealthy. Most were fishermen, small farmers, migrant workers, retired couples, people with low-paying jobs in Miami. They had just enough money to buy or rent a small home. Many lived in trailer parks. Some had no insurance. Now their houses were kindling wood. Their trailer homes looked like crushed soda cans. And with their homes had gone everything they owned, from clothes and furniture to toys and family photographs. Of the houses still standing, most had serious damage.

Shopping centers, warehouses, churches, and schools were ripped out of the ground or hammered into piles of twisted steel beams and splintered wood. Trees littered the ground. Lampposts were bent in two. Street signs were gone, and streets were buried under wreckage. Dogs and cats, horses and cows wandered about, lost.

Help was slow to arrive. The armed forces had planned ahead and were ready to move even before Andrew hit. But civilian leaders were slow to realize how great the damage was slow to ask for help, slow to give orders. Meanwhile, in South Florida some 250,000 people camped out in the ruins as best they could, living with rain and mosquitoes. In all, Andrew had destroyed 20,000 houses and badly damaged another 90,000.

Finally, the troops were given their orders and arrived. Tent cities sprang up. Generators hummed, bringing back electricity. Food and water were supplied. Troops patrolled against looters and directed traffic. Bulldozers and cranes began a giant cleanup. But it would be years before Homestead and Florida City looked like towns again, years before people could put their lives together again.

It would also be years before anyone could tell how plant and animal life had been affected. In the past, many hurricanes have roared across South Florida. Each time, plant and animal life recovered. But in recent years, people have made many changes in the region. Because of these changes, the effects of Andrew's pounding may pose a long-term threat to the ecology of Everglades National Park.

*Andrew tossed a large sailboat into a wooded area and flattened all the trees.*

Like other national parks, Everglades is a piece of wilderness set aside to be preserved in its natural state. But in one way Everglades is unique. Other parks were chosen to preserve landforms. Everglades National Park was to preserve lifeforms. It is a park of birds, mammals, fish, reptiles, and amphibians, and of plants.

Andrew cut through the heart of the park, felling everything in its path. Animals in the park survived well. But in Andrew's winds, slash pines snapped like matchsticks. Gumbo-limbo, wild tamarind, and ancient mahogany trees were uprooted. The storm left behind a tangled mass of dead and dying plants, lying in torn-up ground.

The last hurricane that seriously damaged Everglades swept through in 1960. That time the park recovered well. Some fallen trees re-sprouted. Seeds from similar plants blew in on the winds or were carried in by animals.

Since then many changes have taken place in areas around the park. To the north, land has been drained and cleared for towns, ranches, and farms. The natural flow of water through the park has changed, and chemicals seep into the water. Housing developments have gone up

*With its front wall stripped away by Andrew, a modern apartment building looked like a doll's house.*

right next to the park. And foreign plants have been brought in and planted just outside the park. Among these are Australian pines, Brazilian pepper shrubs, and melaleuca trees. All were brought in as ornamental plants. But they are a

*Melaleuca can spread at a rate of 50 acres a day. It forms dense thickets that crowd out native plants. The melaleuca changes the flow of groundwater, drying up wetlands and driving out native birds, tree frogs, and fish.*

problem. Their seeds spread like wildfire, grow fast, and thrive in disturbed soil. Once they take hold, they are nearly impossible to get rid of.

Before Andrew, the park was under stress because of changes to the north. Now park scientists fear that foreign plants will invade the hurricane-damaged areas, take hold, and drive out native plants. This would change the park's plant life. It would also change the animal life, because animals depend on native plants for food and for places to nest and raise their young.

No one knows how big a change will take place or how it will affect the songbirds and wading birds, the raccoons, bobcats, deer, alligators, snakes, and tree frogs. Park scientists can only wait and see.

Natural scientists are also concerned about damage to mangrove swamps along southern

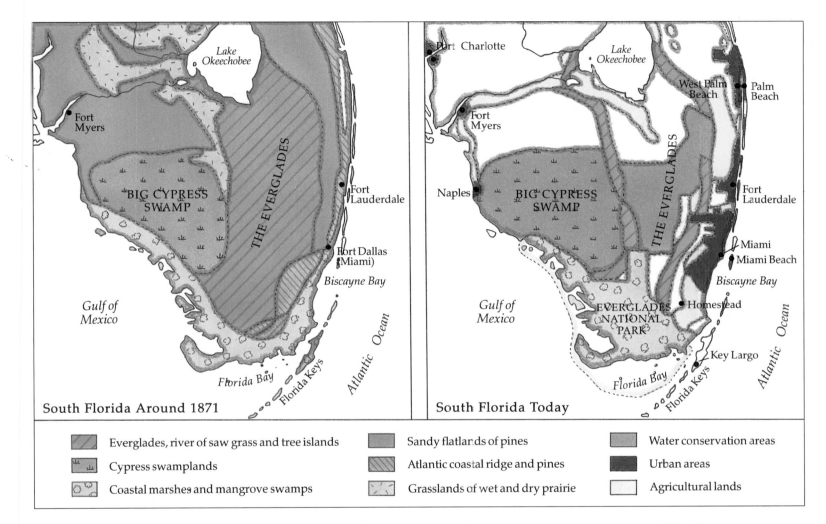

| | | | | | |
|---|---|---|---|---|---|
| Everglades, river of saw grass and tree islands | | Sandy flatlands of pines | | Water conservation areas | |
| Cypress swamplands | | Atlantic coastal ridge and pines | | Urban areas | |
| Coastal marshes and mangrove swamps | | Grasslands of wet and dry prairie | | Agricultural lands | |

*The Everglades was once a region that stretched from Lake Okeechobee to the mangrove swamps at the tip of Florida.
It was a watery land of tall saw grass broken by hammocks, or pieces of higher ground, where hardwood trees grew.
Today Everglades National Park preserves a piece of the Everglades and the many kinds of plants and animals that
live or nest there.*

Biscayne Bay, where Andrew came ashore.

The storm surge spent itself on a string of small barrier islands. But the hurricane's winds and waves battered the shore, which was lined with swamps of mangrove trees. The raging winds shredded the mangroves. When mangroves are lost, many food chains and food webs are affected.

Mangroves are umbrella-shaped trees that can grow in salty water. There are three kinds — the red, the black, and the white. The red is the kind most people are familiar with, because much of its root system is above ground. The roots arch out, like the legs of a crab, around the trunk. They protect the land against ocean storms.

Mangroves are the start of many food chains. These trees shed leaves heavily. The leaves fall in the water, where they become food for bacteria and fungi. The bacteria and fungi are grazed, or fed on, by one-celled animals. All three are eaten by tiny crabs, shrimp, worms, insect young, and small fishes. These animals are in turn eaten by bigger ones — blue crabs, sardines, anchovies,

*Everglades is home to many kinds of birds, among them the roseate spoonbill (top) and the great egret (bottom). The spoonbill feeds by swinging its bill from side to side and straining tiny organisms out of the water and mud.*

*Pelicans, herons, and other birds share the brackish water of a mangrove swamp with an alligator. Unless an alligator is hungry, it poses no threat to other animals.*

eels, sunfish. They are also eaten by young tarpon, snook, gray snapper, spotted sea trout, and others, all of which grow up into big fishes that are at or near the head of food chains. These chains also include other fish eaters, among them alligators, herons, egrets, eagles, wood storks, white ibises, and humans.

Because of the mangroves, the shores are rich in food for many animals. They are also a nursery for the young of many fishes and other sea creatures. They are important to the lives of animals and also to the lives of humans — to those who take their living from the sea and to those who eat food from the sea.

It will be years before anyone can tell how badly Andrew damaged the mangrove swamps and the food chains that begin in them. Florida has lost many miles of mangrove swamps in the past 30 years. They have been filled, cleared, and built on. The remaining ones are precious.

Hurricanes are part of nature. They are natural events. And they have been making landfalls for a very long time. In the past, nature always healed itself after a big blow — plant and animal life came back quickly to damaged areas. Today human activities may have changed the ways in which nature can heal itself. Scientists are concerned about these changes.

They are also concerned about another kind of change: the huge number of people who have moved to coastal areas. The years ahead, scientists say, may see more and more of earth's mightiest storms roaring in from the sea and putting these people at risk.

*A green heron perches on the prop roots of a red mangrove.*

# Iniki: A Hawaiian Storm

Less than three weeks after Hurricane Andrew, another big storm took shape. This one was in the central Pacific and its Hawaiian name was Iniki (ee-NEE-kee), meaning "sharp and piercing." Strong winds were steering it directly toward the islands. Sirens screamed a warning, and people prepared for the worst.

On Friday afternoon, September 11, Iniki came ashore on the island of Kauai (kuh-WYE-ee). Packing winds of 130 miles an hour, with gusts up to 160, it was the most powerful storm to strike Hawaii in this century. When Iniki moved on, more than half the houses on Kauai lay in ruins or had been damaged. Fields and groves of crops were flattened. And the storm had damaged areas of rare native plants.

# Some Other Famous Hurricanes

Nineteen fifty-four was a hurricane year to remember, even though it fell in a period of many hurricanes. In August, Carol, the third hurricane of the season, roared almost straight north from the Bahamas to New England, its eye passing over the eastern end of Long Island. Carol did more property damage than any previous hurricane, but only 60 people died, thanks to an early storm warning.

Less than two weeks later, in early September, Hurricane Edna dumped five inches of rain on New York City in 14 hours, then moved north along Massachusetts and Maine to Nova Scotia. Twenty-two people died.

Worse was to come. In early October one of the most powerful hurricanes ever to pound North America was building up in the Caribbean. On October 12, Hurricane Hazel slammed into Haiti, leveling three towns and killing 1,000 people. The storm was so big that 12 inches of rain drenched Puerto Rico, 500 miles from Haiti.

Hazel curved north, soaking the Bahamas, and crashing onto the U.S. mainland near Myrtle Beach, South Carolina. Wind and waves destroyed every fishing pier for 170 miles along the coast. They tore apart homes, hotels, and office buildings. But because of warnings, only 19 people died.

Although it was now over land, Hazel strengthened. It roared through North Carolina, Virginia, Maryland, Pennsylvania, and New York State, bringing torrents of rain and record winds. Hazel then tore into Canada, dropping seven inches of rain on Toronto and swelling rivers that overflowed and drowned 80 people.

The next year brought two more hurricanes to the Northeast. These 1955 hurricanes did not have high winds and terrible storm surges, but they brought huge amounts of rain. Connie arrived in mid-August. When Diane struck a few days later, the ground had absorbed all the water it could and rivers were already full to overflowing. More than 190 people died, most of them in flooding rivers.

In late July 1957, forecasters had been watching a small but strong hurricane in the Gulf of Mexico. They warned people in low-lying areas to leave. What they did not predict was that the storm, named Audrey, would suddenly speed up and arrive ahead of schedule. When Audrey rushed ashore, people were not ready and 400 died.

In August 1969, weather scientists warned people along the Gulf coast that Camille was an

The name Camille is no longer used for hurricanes. It means only the violent storm that struck the Gulf coast in 1969. In Pass Christian, Mississippi, an entire apartment house fell apart, killing 23 people who had decided to ride out the storm.

extremely dangerous hurricane, tightly packed, with 200-mile-an-hour winds. They expected Camille to come ashore along the Florida panhandle. Instead, the hurricane turned west and struck the Mississippi Delta. A storm surge, 19 feet high, swept through towns, crumbling buildings, and swallowing bridges. Most people had taken the warning seriously and left the coast. But some decided to ride out the storm. Among them were 24 people in an apartment house in Pass Christian, Mississippi. They decided to have a hurricane party and enjoy the excitement. Only one survived, a woman who managed to swim out a window and looked back just in time to see the apartment house collapse. Clinging to wreckage, the woman was blown into a treetop, where she was found the next day.

Hurricane Hugo struck in September 1989. Hugo's winds, waves, and rain leveled houses and felled trees and telephone poles in the Virgin Islands and Puerto Rico, then battered the South Atlantic coast, particularly Charleston, South Carolina.

*The name Hugo is no longer used either. It means only the hurricane that smashed the Virgin Islands before sweeping on to Charleston in 1989.*

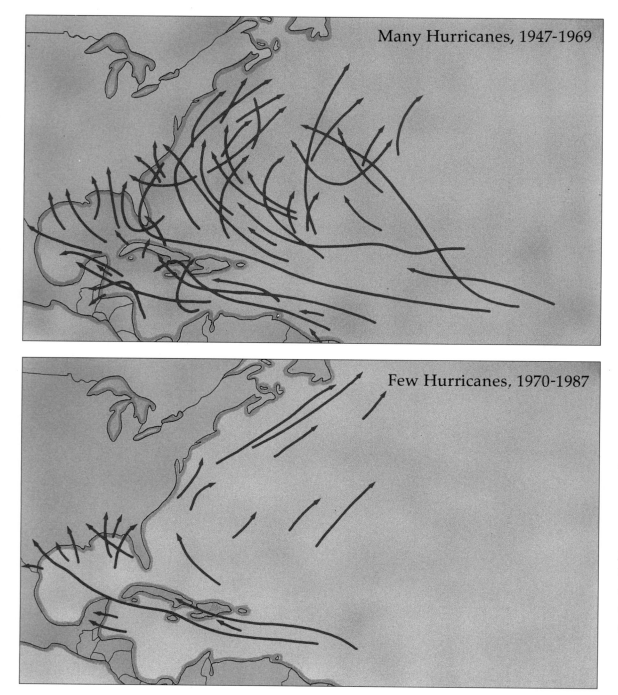

Many Hurricanes, 1947-1969

Few Hurricanes, 1970-1987

HURRICANE CYCLES: *The arrows trace the paths of the strongest hurricanes that occurred during the most recent heavy cycle and the most recent light cycle. The years 1988 through 1994 did not show a clear trend — weather scientists could not tell if they were part of the light cycle or the start of a heavy cycle. The year 1995 brought one of the most active hurricane seasons of this century, but only time will tell if it marked the start of a heavy cycle.*

# MORE STORMS AHEAD?

Hurricanes occur in cycles that last about ten to 20 years. In one cycle many big storms strike the Gulf and East coasts. In the next cycle big storms may blow in, but they are few and far between.

Many weather scientists think that Atlantic hurricanes are linked to rainfall in a region of West Africa. This region is the Sahel, which lies south of the Sahara Desert. When the Sahel suffers years of drought, they say, Atlantic hurricanes are few. When the rains return, so do the hurricanes. The years 1947 through 1969 brought rains to the Sahel. In those same years, 13 hurricanes with winds of more than 110 miles an hour made landfalls in North America. The years 1970 through 1987 brought drought to the Sahel. Only one big hurricane hit. Since 1987 there has been no clear trend. If drought has ended in the Sahel, North America can probably expect more hurricanes. It is possible that 1995 marked the start of a new cycle. It was one of the busiest hurricane years of this century.

During the light cycle, however, more and more people moved toward the shore. Today 44 million people live along the coastline from Maine to Texas. More than 80 percent of them have never experienced a hurricane. Some are too young to have lived through a big blow. Some have moved from inland areas where hurricanes never strike. Even people who have always lived along the coast tend to forget about hurricanes when none occur. They, too, build in places where the sea may come ashore.

As people move to the coast, cities grow. Suburbs spring up around them. Retirement communities take root. Shopping malls edge the highways. Areas that were once open space or farmland become crowded with houses and trailer parks, shops and restaurants. More people face the dangers of hurricanes today than ever before. A big storm will do more property damage than ever before.

What can be done? Over the years many people have wondered if a way might be found to stop or weaken hurricanes. In the late 1940s, tests began to see if this was possible.

A group of scientists experimented first with seeing whether they could make rain or snow fall. Working from an airplane, they seeded clouds with dry ice — frozen carbon dioxide with a temperature of -109.3 degrees. The first three experiments were encouraging. The extreme cold turned water into ice crystals. Snow formed and fell, changing to rain as it met warmer temperatures.

The fourth experiment took place in upstate New York on December 20, 1946. The weather forecast was for "fair and warm." But when a cloud was seeded, the winter's heaviest snow fell on New York and Vermont, blocking roads and causing accidents. It is not known whether the seeding caused the snow, but people in Vermont and New York were not pleased.

Ten months later, an attempt was made to weaken a hurricane. A big storm had struck Miami, then wheeled out to sea. Because it was traveling away from land, it seemed a good hurricane to experiment with. A B-17 bomber seeded it.

By the next day, the hurricane had gathered strength, turned around, and slammed into Savannah, Georgia, causing much damage. Was the seeding to blame? The answer turned out to be no. The storm had already started to change course before the seeding took place. Even so, 11 years passed before another hurricane was seeded.

By then scientists were using silver iodide in place of dry ice. Silver iodide, too, causes ice crystals to form. When they become heavy enough, they fall as snow that becomes rain. The idea was to seed the walls of a hurricane's eye and weaken them. If the walls weakened, the eye would grow and the storm itself would weaken. Several attempts were made to weaken

*Starting in the late 1940s, scientists began sending planes above hurricanes to seed the clouds. They hoped to weaken the storms.*

hurricanes, but only one showed any signs of success — wind speed dropped.

By 1969 almost all work had stopped. A plan to seed typhoons in the Pacific was dropped when China and Japan protested. China feared that experiments would backfire and more typhoons would strike its shores. Japan feared that the experiments would succeed and cut off the typhoon rains that the country needed. Then too, many scientists were having second thoughts about trying to change the weather.

Hurricanes help to exchange hot air from the equator for cold air from the polar regions. They carry away dirty air and bring in fresh air.

*The path of the plane that seeded these hurricane clouds can be seen in this photograph. This experiment was a success. Seeding caused droplets of water in the clouds to form ice crystals, which fell as a snow shower.*

Their clouds carry rain that may be needed. If hurricanes were tamed, there is no way of knowing what else might change — only that change would take place. And the change might cause far more damage than the storms.

Even without stopping hurricanes, much can

be done to make life safer for people who are at risk.

Forecasters have already taken great strides forward. Their warnings have saved countless lives. And the more they learn about hurricanes, the safer people will be.

Life is also made safer when towns, counties, and states plan ahead, setting up ways to evacuate people and providing safe places to go. Warnings do not help much if there is nowhere to go or roads are choked with cars.

All hurricane areas need good building codes — and lots of inspectors to make sure the codes are followed. Around Homestead, many developers did not follow the building code. They used poor materials and did not attach roofs properly. With only a few building inspectors, the problems were not found and corrected. That was one reason Andrew did great damage.

Some areas must take special steps to protect themselves. One of these is New Orleans, which lies six feet below sea level and is mostly bordered by water. The city has built a flood wall, eight and a half miles long, to hold back lakes that could send 20 feet of water into the city during

## How People Can Help Themselves

There are many things people can do to help themselves if they live where hurricanes strike. An easy one is to pay attention to weather reports during the hurricane season, which starts in June and may last until December.

If a hurricane appears to be heading for land, the National Hurricane Center sends out a *hurricane watch*. This means that a hurricane may hit land, but not right away. It's a good time to check the batteries in flashlights and radios, to fill cars with gas, and to lay in supplies of food and water.

A *hurricane warning* means that a hurricane is likely to strike within the next 24 hours. People who live in low-lying areas may be told to evacuate — to leave for some place safer. They should do so at once. Being caught in hurricane-lashed seas and mighty winds is both dangerous and terrifying.

a big hurricane. But the city needs a stronger building code and many more inspectors.

No hurricane will ever again come as a terrifying surprise, as the 1938 storm did. Satellites, hurricane-hunting planes, radar, and computers make sure of that. But hurricanes are part of nature and they will occur in the years ahead. Small storms will start, somewhere over tropical waters. Feeding on warm, moist air, they will grow. Spiraling winds will howl within their clouds and rain will fall in sheets. The small storms will grow and gather strength. They will become earth's mightiest storms — hurricanes.

*The year 1995 saw many storms. In early October, Hurricane Roxanne came ashore on the Gulf coast of Mexico, went back to sea, weakened, then picked up strength and returned to hit some areas a second time. Thousands of people were forced from their homes by flooding and much damage was done to cattle ranches and banana plantations.*

The western Pacific also had a busy storm season in 1995. By the end of October, weather scientists had used up their alphabet of names and had to start over again when Typhoon Angela hit the Philippines in early November. The worst storm in ten years, it sent 200,000 people fleeing to escape flash floods and toppling buildings.

# INDEX

*Italics* indicate photo only.

# FURTHER READING

★ *indicates a book that is suitable for more advanced readers.*

## HURRICANES AND STORMS

Archer, Jules, *Hurricane!* New York: Crestwood House, 1991.

Dineen, Jacqueline, *Hurricanes and Typhoons.* New York: Franklin Watts, 1991.

Kahl, Jonathan D., *Storm Warning.* Minneapolis: Lerner Publications, 1993.

Lee, Sally, *Hurricanes.* New York: Franklin Watts, 1993.

Twist, Clint, *Hurricanes and Storms.* New York: New Discovery, 1992.

★ Whipple, A.B.C., *Storm.* Alexandria, Virginia: Time-Life Books, 1982.

## WEATHER

Ardley, N., *The Science Book of Weather.* San Diego: Harcourt Brace Jovanovich, 1992.

Cosgrove, Brian, *Weather.* New York: Alfred A. Knopf, 1991.

McVey, Vicki, *The Sierra Club Book of Weatherwisdom.* Boston: Little Brown, 1991.

## EVERGLADES NATIONAL PARK

★ Caulfield, Patricia, *Everglades.* San Francisco: Sierra Club, 1970.

George, Jean Craighead, *The Everglades.* New York: HarperCollins, 1992.

Lauber, Patricia, *Everglades Country.* New York: The Viking Press, 1973.

★ Toops, Connie, *Everglades.* Stillwater, Minnesota: Voyageur Press, 1989.

# PICTURE CREDITS

Front cover and p. 53: © Gary Williams/Gamma-Liaison; back cover and p. 34: © NASA/Weatherstock; title page: © M. Laca/Weatherstock; contents page: © Rosenburg Library, Galveston, Texas.

A MONSTER STORM: p. 6: © Leo De Wys Inc.; p. 9: © AP/Wide World; p. 11: © UPI/Bettmann; p. 12: © Connecticut Historical Society, Hartford; p. 13: © Connecticut Historical Society, Hartford; p. 14: © Adler's Photo, Providence; p. 15: © Connecticut Historical Society, Hartford; p. 16: © Westfield Congregational Church, Connecticut; p. 17: © Frank Jo Raymond/Westerly Sun Glass Plate Collection.

THE MAKING OF A HURRICANE: p. 24: © UPI/Bettmann; p. 26, top right and left, bottom right: © Taylor Environmental Instruments; p. 26, bottom left: © Warren Faidley/Weatherstock.

INTO THE EYE OF THE STORM: p. 28: © U.S. Air Force/Science Service; p. 30: NOAA; p. 31: NOAA; p. 32: © Warren Faidley/Picture Group; p. 34: NASA.

BIG WINDS AND BIG DAMAGE: p. 36: © Weatherstock; p. 39: © Ray Fairall/AP/Wide World; p. 40, left: © Raul Demolina/Sygma; p. 40, right: © Jeff Cory/Sipa-Press; p. 42: © Patrick Farrell/*Miami Herald*; p. 43: © J. Berry/Gamma-Liaison; p. 44: © Claudine Laabs; p. 46, top: © Ralph A. Reinhold/Animals Animals; p. 46, bottom: © Ken Cole/Animals Animals; p. 47: © Peter Weimann/Animals Animals; p. 48: © Robert A. Lubeck/ Animals Animals; p. 49: © Keith Karasic/Black Star; p. 51: © Chauncey Hinman.

MORE STORMS AHEAD?: p. 57: © Archive Photos; p. 58: © General Electric Hall of History; pp. 60-61: © Dario Lopez-Mills/AP/Wide World; p. 61, right: © Fernando Sepe, Jr./AP/Wide World; p. 64: © AP/Wide World.

The author expresses her sincere thanks to Dr. Walter A. Robinson, Associate Professor of Atmospheric Sciences, University of Illinois, for his helpful suggestions and expert advice about hurricanes.